THE SEVEN VIRTUES

The Seven Last Words and
The Art of Practicing Virtue

FULTON J. SHEEN

Bishop Sheen Today
280 John Street
Midland, Ontario, Canada
L4R 2J5

www.bishopsheentoday.com

Library of Congress Cataloging-in-Publication Data

Names: Sheen, Fulton J. (Fulton John), 1895-1979, author. | Smith, Allan J., editor.

Sheen, Fulton J. (Fulton John), 1895-1979. The Seven Virtues. - Registered in the name of P.J. Kenedy & Sons, under Library of Congress catalog card number: A139984 following publication April 26, 1940.

Smith, Al (Allan J.) editor – The Cries of Jesus from the Cross: A Fulton Sheen Anthology. Manchester, New Hampshire: Sophia Institute Press, 2018, ISBN 9781622826209.

Title: The Seven Virtues: The Seven Last Words and the Art of Practicing Virtue

Fulton J. Sheen; compiled by Allan J. Smith.

Description: Midland, Ontario:Bishop Sheen Today, 2021

Includes bibliographical references.

Identifiers: ISBN: 978-1-998229-37-6 (paperback)
ISBN: 978-1-7371890-0-8 (eBook)

ISBN: 978-1-990-427-74-9 (hardcover)

Subjects: Jesus Christ — The Seven Last Words — The Virtues

DEDICATED TO

**Mary Immaculate
Mother of God**

IN TOKEN OF FILIAL
GRATITUDE AND AFFECTION

*Ad maiorem Dei gloriam
inque hominum salute*

Jesus calls all His children to the pulpit of the Cross, and every word He says to them is set down for the purpose of an eternal publication and undying consolation.

There was never a preacher like the dying Christ.

There was never a congregation like that which gathered about the pulpit of the Cross.

And there was never a sermon like the Seven Last Words.

Archbishop Fulton J. Sheen

THE SEVEN LAST WORDS OF CHRIST

The First Word
"Father, Forgive Them For They

Know Not What They Do."

The Second Word
"This Day Thou Shalt

Be With Me In Paradise."

The Third Word
"Woman, Behold Thy Son;

Behold Thy Mother."

The Fourth Word
"My God! My God!

Why Hast Thou Forsaken Me?"

The Fifth Word
"I Thirst."

The Sixth Word
"It Is Finished."

The Seventh Word
"Father, Into Thy Hands

I Commend My Spirit."

CONTENTS

PREFACE

*"I have learned more from the
crucifix than from any book."*

St. Thomas Aquinas

ARCHBISHOP FULTON J. SHEEN was a man for all seasons. Over his lifetime, he spent himself for souls, transforming lives with the clear teaching of the truths of Christ and His Church through his books, his radio addresses, his lectures, his television series, and his many newspaper columns.

The topics of this much-sought-after lecturer ranged from the social concerns of the day to matters of faith and morals. With an easy and personable manner, Sheen could strike up a conversation on just about any subject, making numerous friends as well as converts.

During the 1930s and '40s, Fulton Sheen was the featured speaker on The Catholic Hour radio broadcast, and millions of listeners heard his radio addresses each week. His topics ranged from politics and the economy to philosophy and man's eternal pursuit of happiness.

Along with his weekly radio program, Sheen wrote dozens of books and pamphlets. One can safely say that through his writings, thousands of people changed their perspectives about God and the Church. Sheen was quoted as saying, "There are not one hundred people in the United States who hate the Catholic Church, but there are millions who hate what they wrongly perceive the Catholic Church to be."

Possessing a burning zeal to dispel the myths about Our Lord and His Church, Sheen gave a series of powerful presentations on Christ's Passion and His seven last words from the Cross. As a Scripture scholar, Archbishop Sheen knew full well the power contained in preaching Christ crucified. With St. Paul, he could say, "For I decided to know nothing among you except Jesus Christ and him crucified" (1 Cor. 2:2).

During his last recorded Good Friday address in 1979, Archbishop Sheen spoke of having given this type of reflection on the subject of Christ's seven last words from the Cross "for the fifty-eighth consecutive time." Whether from the young priest in Peoria, Illinois, the university professor in Washington, D.C., or the bishop in New York, Sheen's messages were sure to make an indelible mark on his listeners.

Given their importance and the impact they had on society, it seemed appropriate to bring back this collection of Sheen's radio addresses that were later compiled into a book titled The Seven Virtues (New York: P.J. Kenedy and Sons, 1940).

On October 2, 1979, when visiting St. Patrick's Cathedral in New York City, Pope John Paul II embraced Fulton Sheen and spoke into his ear a blessing and an affirmation. He said: "You have written and spoken well of the Lord Jesus Christ. You are a loyal son of the Church." On the day Archbishop Sheen died (December 9, 1979), he was found in his private chapel before the Eucharist in the shadow of the cross. Archbishop Sheen was a man purified in the fires of love and by the wood of the Cross.

It is hoped that, upon reading these reflections, the reader will concur with the heartfelt affirmation given by St. John Paul II and countless others of Sheen's wisdom and fidelity. May these writings by Archbishop Fulton J. Sheen evoke a greater love and appreciation for the seven virtues of Fortitude, Hope, Prudence, Faith, Temperance, Justice, and Charity.

INTRODUCTION

THESE MEDITATIONS on the Seven Last Words correlated to the seven virtues make no pretence to absoluteness. The Words are not necessarily related to the virtues but they do make convenient points of illustrations.

This book has only one aim: to awaken a love in the Passion of Our Lord and to incite the practice of virtue. If it does that in but one soul its publication has been justified.

THE FIRST VIRTUE

- *Fortitude* -

"Father, forgive them, for they know not what they do."

THERE IS ENTIRELY too much psycho-analysis in the world; what is needed is a little more psycho-synthesis. Hearts and minds have been analyzed to a point where they are nothing more than a chaotic mass of unrelated nerve impulses. There is need for someone to pull them together, to give them a pattern of life and above all, peace. The pattern around which we shall psycho-synthesize all these soul-states will be the Cross.

Here we are interested in three types of souls: a) Those who suffer and mourn, saying "What have I done to deserve this?"; b) those who possess faith, but who through a love of the world deny their faith or hide it; c) and those who do not possess the faith, but are convinced of its truth and yet refuse to pay the price.

There is a virtue, which these three types of souls need for their peace, and that is the virtue of Fortitude.

Fortitude may be defined as that virtue, which enables us to face undismayed and fearlessly the difficulties, and dangers which stand in the way of duty and goodness. It stands midway between foolhardiness, which rushes into danger heedlessly, and cowardice, which flees from it recreantly. Because fortitude is related to bravery, it must not be thought that bravery is devoid of fear; rather it is control of fear. Fortitude is of two kinds, depending upon whether it is directed to a natural good or a supernatural good.

A soldier, for example, who braves the dangers of battle for love of country practices natural fortitude. But the saint who overcomes all difficulties and dangers for the sake of the glory of God and the salvation of his soul practices supernatural fortitude.

It is in the presence of the fear of death that Fortitude reaches its peak; that is why the highest peak of supernatural fortitude is martyrdom. We are here concerned only with supernatural fortitude.

This virtue reaches its peak in practice in the life of Our Divine Lord: He was primarily a Redeemer — God in the form of man saving men of whom He was King and Captain. "For God sent not his Son into the world, to judge the world, but that the world may be saved by him" (John 3:17).

His baptism was death, and He was "straitened until it be accomplished" (Luke 12:50). Being truly a man, He felt the fear every normal man feels in the face of danger. "If it be possible, let this chalice pass from Me" (Matthew 26:39); but resigned to the Father's business, He added: "Nevertheless not as I will, but as thou wilt" (Matthew 26:39).

No difficulty, however great, would deter Him from the Divine purpose of laying down His life for the redemption of many. Not even "twelve legions of Angels" (Matthew 26:53) would He permit to solace Him in His darkest hour, and not even a drug would He touch to His lips to deaden the pains of the Cross.

Solomon of old had said: "Give strong drink to them that are sad, and wine to them that are grieved in mind: Let them drink and forget their want, and remember their sorrow no more" (Proverbs 31:6,7).

The Talmud says it was the custom to put a grain of incense in the draft of those who were being led to death, to deaden the sense of pain.

This intoxicating draft, which was given Him as His hands and feet, were nailed to a tree of His own creation, He refused to drink (Matthew 27:34). He strides forth boldly to the high things of God. He will meet death in the full possession of His faculties — fearlessly.

But not in this was His fortitude greatest: when death is upon Him by His own submission, for "no man taketh it away from me: but I lay it down of myself" (John 10:18), His first word from the Cross is not in self-defense, not a protestation of His own innocence, not a fear of death nor a plea for deliverance, nor even fear of enemies.

Fear of death makes most men turn away from doing good. It makes even innocent men thoughtful of themselves as they proclaim their innocence to their executioners. Not so with Him. Fortitude reaches the peak of self-forgetfulness. On the Cross, He thinks only of others and their salvation.

For His first word is not about death, but about the good it will accomplish; it is directed not to His friends, His Apostles, or His believers who will proclaim His gospel, but to those who hate Him and His Apostles and His Church: "Father, forgive them, for they know not what they do" (Luke 23:34).

Often during His life, He preached: "Love your enemies: do good to them that hate you" (Matthew 5:44). Now that He is strong enough to ignore death, He the Conqueror bestows on

His momentary conquerors the very thing they had forfeited by their sins — forgiveness.

Why is it that He appeals to His Father to forgive, and does not Himself forgive directly? Because He is looking at the crucifixion not from the human point of view, but from the Divine. They were wronging the Father by killing His Divine Son. The crucifixion is not murder; it is deicide.

Murder is a sin against God Who gave human life to human care. Deicide is a sin against God Who entrusted Divine Life to human love. It was not the candle of a man's life the executioners were snuffing out; it was the sun they were trying to extinguish.

The noon-day sun never darkened on murder, but it hid its face in shame as the Light of the World went into the momentary eclipse of death.

No stronger proclamation of His Divinity could have been uttered than for the Divine Son to ask the Divine Father to forgive the sons of men for their Golgothas, their swastikas, and their hammers and sickles. If He were only a man, He would have asked His own forgiveness, but being God, He asked His Father for the pardon of men.

Scripture does not record that anyone except the Thief on the right, within the hearing of that cry, repented or even regretted driving the nails and unfurling the flag of the Cross to the four winds of the world. There is not a single record that anyone else expressed a desire to follow Him or that they were touched by His calmness under fire.

Thus the world's greatest act of bravery when He who was thoughtless of self became thoughtful of others, went momentarily barren. They were apparently satisfied to sit and watch.

But it was for a bigger world than Calvary that He died, and for greater harvests than Jerusalem that He suffered. "And not for them only do I pray, but for them also who through their word shall believe in me" (John 17:20).

Now that the Divine Physician has prepared the medicine apply it to the first of our three types of souls, namely, those who suffer and mourn saying: "What have I done to deserve this?"

There are many good men and women tossing on beds of pain, their bodies wasted by long sickness, their hearts broken with woe and sorrow, or their minds tortured by the irreparable loss of friends and fortune. If these souls want peace, they must recognize that in this world there is no intrinsic connection between personal sin and suffering.

One day "Jesus passing by, saw a man, who was blind from his birth: And his disciples asked him: Rabbi, who hath sinned, this man, or his parents, that he should be born blind? Jesus answered: Neither hath this man sinned nor his parents" (John 9:1-3).

That brings us face to face with the inscrutable will of God which we cannot understand, any more than a mouse in a piano can understand why a musician disturbs him by playing. Our puny minds cannot understand the mysteries of God. But there are two basic truths, which such burdened souls, must never surrender. Otherwise, they will never find peace. First, God is love.

Hence anything He does to me deserves my gratitude, and I will say "thank you." God is still good even though He does not give me whatever I want in this world. He gives me only what I need for the next.

Parents do not give five-year-old boys guns to play with, though there is hardly a boy of five who does not want a gun. As Job put it: "If we have received good things at the hand of God, why should we not receive evil?" (Job 2:10).

Second, the final reward for virtue comes not in this life, but in the next. As tapestries are woven not from the front but from the back, so too in this life we see only the underside of God's plan.

"My life is but a weaving
Between my God and me.
I may but choose the colors
He worketh skilfully.

Full oft He chooses sorrow,
And I, in foolish pride,
Forget He sees the upper,
And I the under, side."

Father Tabb

We are not to have our moods made by the world; the world should revolve about us; not us about the world. Like the earth in its revolution about the sun, we will carry our own atmosphere with us — resignation to the will of God. Then nothing can ever happen against our will because our will is the will of God.

This is not fatalism, which is subjection to blind necessity; it is patience, which is resignation to the will of the Divine Love who in the end can desire nothing but the eternal happiness and perfection of the one loved.

Fatalism is nonsense as the man walking precariously on the railing of a ship in a stormy sea proved when he said to the worried onlookers: "I'm a fatalist."

But patient resignation is exemplified by the child who said to her father: "Daddy, I do not know why you want me to go to the hospital for that operation. It hurts. I know only that you love me."

The shock of sorrow comes only to those who think this world is fixed and absolute, that there is nothing beyond. They think everything here below should be perfect. Hence they ask questions: "Why should I suffer? What have I done to deserve this?" Maybe you did nothing to deserve it. Certainly, Our Lord did nothing to deserve His Cross. But it came, and through it, He went to His glory.

The virtue to be cultivated then by such souls is what is known as Patience. Patience and Fortitude are related as the convex and concave sides of a saucer. Fortitude is exercised in the active struggle with dangers and difficulties, while Patience is the passive acceptance of what is hard to bear.

Our Lord on the Cross practiced Fortitude by freely and fearlessly meeting death to purchase our forgiveness; He practiced

Patience by passively accepting the Father's will.

Being God, He could have stepped down from the Cross. Twelve legions of angels could have ministered to His wounds; the earth could have been His footstool, the seas as healing balm, the sun as His chariot, the planets His cortège, and the Cross His triumphal throne. But He willed to accept death to give us an example: "Not my will, but thine be done" (Luke 22:42).

Passive acceptance of God's will is Patience. Patience, other things being equal, is nobler than Fortitude; for in active works we may choose what pleases us and thereby sometimes deceive ourselves, but in resignation, to the crosses of life it is always God's will that we do.

"In your patience," He said, "you shall possess your souls" (Luke 21:19). In His Patience, He possesses His, for He did not choose His Cross, it was made for Him. He was fitted and patterned to it; we might almost say cut to fit it.

To take the Cross God sends us as He took the one given to Him, even though we do not deserve it, is the shortest way to identification with God's will which is the beginning of Power and Peace: Power because we are one with Him who can do all things; Peace because we are tranquil in the love of Him who is just.

Dare we call ourselves Christian and expect another road to heaven than that which Christ Himself traveled? Love leads the way — it is enough for us to follow the Beloved knowing that He loves and cares. Then instead of seeking to have a road free of obstacles to attain God, we shall, like hurdles in the race of life, make a race out of obstacles.

Embracing the crosses of life because given to us by Love on the Cross, does not mean that any of us ever reach the stage where our nature is willing to suffer. On the contrary, our nature rebels against it because it is contrary to nature. But we can will supernaturally what nature rejects, just as our reason can accept what the senses reject.

My eyes tell me I should not let the doctor lance the festering boil, for it will hurt. But my reason tells me that my senses must momentarily submit to the pain for the sake of a future good. So too we can will to bear the unavoidable ills of life for supernatural reasons. The First Word from the Cross suggests doing so for the sake of the remission of sins: "Forgive them."

In the business world, we contract debts and recognize our obligation and duty to acquit them. Why should we think that in the same moral universe we can sin with impunity? If then we bear the imprints of the Cross, instead of complaining against God let us occasionally think of offering them up to God for our own sins, or for the sins of our neighbors.

Of all the nonsense our modern world has invented, nothing surpasses the catchwords or claptrap we give the unfortunate or the sick: "Keep your chin up" or "Forget it." This is not solace, but a drug. Consolation is in explaining suffering, not forgetting it; in relating it to Love, not ignoring it; in making it an expiation for sin, not another sin. But who shall understand this unless he looks at a Cross and loves the Crucified?

The second type of soul who can be helped by this First Word from the Cross is he who, possessing the great gift of Faith, out of love of the world either hides it or denies it. This applies to those lukewarm Catholics who say: "Of course I ate meat at the party on Friday. Did you think I was going to have everyone laughing at me?" "Yes, I sent my son to a non-Catholic college. They are more social you know, and I don't want my boy to meet policemen's sons." Or, "When that chap at the office ridiculed the

Mass, I did not say I was a Catholic, for the boss is anti-Catholic, and I might lose my job."

Doubtlessly such spineless Catholics would fit the spirit of the world better if they gave up their faith. Business men could then meet the challenge of chiseling competitors; the passion of youth could have its fling; husbands could have second wives; wives could have third husbands; both husbands and wives could find an alternative to self-restraint and thus escape the comparative poverty attendant upon raising a family; politicians could improve their chances for election if they were less Catholic; lawyers could be richer if they did not have to confess their sins and make amends; doctors could be wealthier if they were less conscientious and ceased to believe in Divine Justice.

There is no challenging the fact that Catholics could get on better with the world if they were less Catholic.

Not a single sentence can be found in the words of our Divine Lord promising you the love of the world because of your faith. But you can find a golden string of texts warning you that the world will hate you because you are His: "If you had been of the world, the world would love its own: but because you are not of the world, but I have chosen you out of the world, therefore the world hateth you" (John 15:19).

"Everyone therefore that shall confess me before men, I will also confess him before my Father who is in heaven. But he that shall deny me before men, I will also deny him before my Father who is in heaven . . . And he that taketh not up his cross, and followeth me, is not worthy of me. He that findeth his life shall lose it and he that shall lose his life for me, shall find it" (Matthew 10:32-33, 38-39).

"How narrow is the gate, and strait is the way that leadeth to life: and few there are that find it" (Matthew 7:14).

"For he that shall be ashamed of me, and of my words, in this adulterous and sinful generation: the Son of man also will be ashamed of him, when he shall come in the glory of his Father with the holy angels" (Mark 8:38; Cf. Luke 9:26).

"If we suffer, we shall also reign with him. If we deny him, he will also deny us" (2 Timothy 2:12).

"And if thy right hand scandalize thee, cut it off, and cast it from thee: for it is expedient for thee that one of thy members should perish, rather than that thy whole body go into hell" (Matthew 5:30).

The true followers of Christ were meant to be at odds with the world: The pure of heart will be laughed at by the Freudians; the meek will be scorned by the Marxists; the humble will be walked on by the go-getters; the liberal Sadducees will call them reactionaries; the reactionary Pharisees will call them liberals.

And Our Lord so warned: "Blessed are ye when they shall revile you, and persecute you, and speak all that is evil against you, untruly, for my sake: Be glad and rejoice for your reward is very great in heaven. For so they persecuted the prophets that were before you" (Matthew 5:11).

To all those compromising Catholics, a plea is made to practice the Fortitude of the Saviour on the Cross who, being thoughtless of death for the sake of our forgiveness, taught us to be thoughtless of the world's scorn for the sake of being forgiven.

We must not forget the word of Our Saviour: "He that shall deny me before men, I will also deny him before my Father who is in heaven" (Matthew 10:33). And if Catholics will not be strong in their love of Christ because of Christ, then let them be strong out of fear of the scandal of their weakness.

The example of a bad Catholic is most often appealed to as a justification for evil. Why is it that the world is more scandalized at a bad Catholic than a bad anything else if it be not because his fall is rightfully measured by the heights from which he has fallen.

And let this fortitude be not a muscular fortitude or abusive fortitude, but a fortitude brave enough to declare the belief in God even among the enemies who nail us to the cross of scorn, a fortitude like unto that of Eleazar, who, when commanded by Antiochus the enemy of the Jews to eat forbidden meat and who was advised by his own friends to do so, answered: "It doth not become our age . . . to dissemble . . . Though, for the present time, I should be delivered from the punishments of men, yet should I not escape the hand of the Almighty neither alive nor dead" (2 Maccabees 6:24, 26).

The third type of soul to whom this First Word offers Fortitude comprises those who are convinced of the truth of the faith but are unwilling to pay the price. A price does have to be paid for conversion, and that price is scorn. Many souls stand poised between an inner conviction that the Church is true and the certitude that if they embrace it, they must make enemies.

Once they cross its threshold a thinly veiled hostility often takes the place of friendship. They may be accused of having lost their reason; their jobs may be endangered; their friends who believed in freedom of conscience may now turn against them because their consciences acted freely; their love of liturgy will be scorned, as superstition and their supernatural faith will be called credulity.

If they joined a crazy cult or became a sun-worshipper or a Yogi follower or founded a new religion, their friends would say they acted within their constitutional rights; but when they join the Church, some will say they lost their minds, as they told Our Lord He had a devil.

Why this revolution of attitude once the threshold of the Church has been passed? Very simply because entering into the Church lifts us into another world — the supernatural world. It gives us a new set of values, a new objective, new ways of thinking, new standards of judgment, all of which are in opposition to the spirit of the world.

The world with its hatred of discipline, its courtesy to the flesh, and its indifference to truth cannot tolerate a life based upon the primacy of Christ and the salvation of souls. "I have chosen you out of the world, therefore the world hateth you. If you had been of the world, the world would love its own . . . [but] know ye, that it hath hated me before you" (John 15:19, 18).

Most people today want a religion which suits the way they live, rather than one which makes demands upon them. The result is that in order to make religion popular, too many prophets have watered down religion until it is hardly distinct from sentimental secularism. Religion thus becomes a luxury like an opera, not a responsibility like life.

There is no doubt that a religion which makes concessions to human weakness will be popular; for example, one that denies hell for those who are unjust, and is silent about divorce for those who have repudiated their vows.

But as Catholics, we may not tamper with the message of Christ; for religion is of His making, not ours. Furthermore, the only religion which will help the world is one which contradicts the world.

Most Americans have been so disillusioned by a Cross-less Christ, that they are now looking back to the Cross as the only point of reference which gives meaning to life. They may not know how to phrase the conflict within, but they dimly perceive that all unhappiness is due to a conflict of wills: Family quarrels arise that way; misery of souls arises that way too when our selfish will contradicts the Divine will.

Peace, we are just discovering, is in the identity of our will with God who wills our perfection. When we disobey His will we are not asserting our independence; we are mutilating our personality as we might mutilate a razor by using it to cut a tree. Being made for God, we can be happy only with Him.

All our misery is traceable to that rebellion. All our peace is traceable to training the lower part of ourselves in service to Him. Hence the Cross, the symbol of that sacrifice inspired by love.

THE SECOND VIRTUE

- Hope -

"This day thou shalt be with me in paradise."

OUR CONCERN PRESENTLY is with two kinds of souls; the despairing and the presumptuous: either those who say, "I am too wicked for God to be interested in me," or those who say, "Oh, I need not worry about my sins. God will take good care of me in the end."

Both these statements are sins of exaggeration. The first is the sin of despair, which exaggerates Divine Justice; the second is the sin of presumption, which exaggerates Divine Mercy. Somewhere there is a golden mean where "Justice and mercy kiss" as the Psalmist puts it, and that is the virtue of Hope.

The virtue of Hope is quite different from the emotion of Hope. The emotion centers in the body and is a kind of dreamy desire that we can be saved without much effort. The virtue of Hope, however, is centered in the will and may be defined as a divinely infused disposition of the will by which with sure confidence, thanks to the powerful help of Almighty God, we expect to pursue eternal happiness, using all the means necessary for attaining it.

The virtue of Hope lies not in the future of time, but beyond the tomb in eternity; its object is not the abundant life of earth, but the eternal love of God.

No stage was ever better set for the drama of Hope than Calvary. Seven centuries before, Isaias had prophesied that Our Divine Lord would be numbered with the wicked. In this hour the prophecy is fulfilled as two thieves, like unholy courtiers, stand unwilling guard on the King of Kings. Nothing could better reveal the contempt in which the Son of God was held than to have crucified Him between two common thieves.

To this ridicule of unholy companionship was added the mockery of a parade that passed before the throne of the central Cross. The Evangelists note them as they pass: rulers, soldiers, and passersby. "And the people stood beholding, and the rulers with them derided him, saying: He saved others; let him save himself if he be Christ, the elect of God" (Luke 23:35). "And the soldiers also mocked him, coming to him, and offering him vinegar" (Luke 23:36). "And they that passed by, blasphemed him, wagging their heads, and saying: Vah, thou that destroyest the temple of God, and in three days dost rebuild it; save thy own self; and if thou be the Son of God, come down from the cross" (Matthew 27:39-40).

As one gazes on that spectacle of three crosses silhouetted against a black and frightened sky, one sees in prospect the future judgment of the world; the Judge in the center and the two divisions of humanity on either side: The sheep and the goats; the blessed and the lost; those who love and those who hate; for the end shall be as the beginning, except that Christ shall appear for the final judgment not on the cross of ignominy but with the cross in glory in the clouds of heaven.

The spiritual development of the thief on the right, reveals how hope is born first out of fear, then out of faith. His conversion began the moment he feared. Like the thief on the left, he too had blasphemed that Man on the central Cross. Then suddenly turning his head he shouted across the face of Divine Mercy, to his blaspheming fellow thief: "Neither dost thou fear God, seeing thou art under the same condemnation? And we indeed justly, for we receive the due reward of our deeds; but this man hath done no evil" (Luke 23:40-41).

The fear of God of which this robber spoke was not a servile fear that God would punish them for their thefts; it was rather a filial fear based on reverence — a fear of displeasing Him who had done nothing to deserve such a humiliating death.

There is the first lesson: Hope begins with fear; hope involves fear because Hope is not certainty. We can, of course, be certain God will help us and give us sufficient strength to be saved, but we cannot be sure that we will always be faithful to His Grace.

God will not fail us; we need have no fear on that score. But we may fail God. The certitude that I am on the way to God does not exclude the fear that through some fault of mine, I may not come to His Blessed Presence.

Note the next step toward hope in the good thief as his fear led to faith, for "The fear of the Lord . . . is wisdom" (Job 28:28).

In a single moment, a soul with a genuine fear of God can come to a greater understanding of the purpose of life than in a lifetime spent in the study of the ephemeral philosophies of men. That is why death-bed conversions may be sincere conversions. The hardened soul disbelieves in God until that awful moment when he has no one to deceive but himself. Once the spark of salutary fear of God had jumped into the soul of the thief from the flaming furnace of that central Cross, fear gave way to faith. His next words were believing.

No longer was Christ an innocent man, nor an exiled upstart, nor a mock monarch. He was a King! Those thorns were His crown; that Cross was His throne; He had Omnipotent Power; that nail was His scepter; He was a Saviour — that is why He forgave His enemies.

Out from the full heart of the thief, there welled up the hopeful petition: "Remember me when thou shalt come into thy kingdom" (Luke 23:42). He could not desire what he did not know; he could not hope in what he did not believe. The thief had faith in the Son of God; now he could hope.

And that hope born of fear and faith received its immediate response: "This day thou shalt be with me in paradise" (Luke 23:43).

Above the blasphemous, raucous background of others shouting "Himself He cannot save," he heard: "This Day." He had only asked for the future, but the answer was more than he had hoped: "This Day." His arms were still pinioned, but he felt them loosen at the sound of "This Day"; his body was still racked by pain, but he felt it freshen at "This Day." His life was of little value — but his soul took on eternal worth as he heard "This Day . . . Paradise." A thief had learned to call "Lord" to

One whom he despised. And the Lord can forgive sins . . . Such is the beginning of Hope.

Two thieves there were: One who loved and one who hated. Each was on a cross. Neither the good nor the bad ever escape the cross. One thief was saved; therefore, let no one despair. One thief was lost; therefore, let no one presume.

The two extremes to be avoided then are presumption and despair. Presumption is an excess of hope, and despair is a defect of hope. Presumption is an inordinate trust in Divine Mercy, a hope of pardon without repentance, a heaven without merit.

A word to the presumptuous who hope for a death-bed conversion to make their peace with God, and who say: "God would not send me to hell," or "I have lived a fairly decent life, so I have nothing to worry about," or "I know I am a sinner, but no worse than my neighbor; why should I worry? God is merciful."

When you make the statement "God is good," what do you mean? Only this: "God is insensible to evil. He is good because He is unmindful of my wickedness." You forget that God is good precisely because He is the enemy of evil. A healthy man is not indifferent to disease; nor is a government good because it ignores crimes and injustice. Why then should you think that God will be complacent about that which you refuse to accept in others?

If you really believed that God is good, would you not be scrupulous about offending Him? Do you not do that much for your friends? The nobler a person is, the more you dread offending him. Even for those whom you do not love, you show respect.

Will you then exploit Divine Goodness and deceive One in whom you repose the confidence of salvation? Will you forget that Goodness wounded by cynicism avenges itself?

If you lose your earthly friends by prostituting their generosity, will you not in like manner lose your Heavenly Friend by presuming? Will you make Divine Mercy the excuse for greater sinning? ls, there not in every life a last pardon as there is also a last sin? Have we not allotted to each of us a final sin, which fills up the "bag of sin" and seals our eternity?

You may sin a thousand times and be forgiven, but like the man who threw himself into a river a hundred times, each time to be rescued by the bridge-tender, you may be told by the rescuer: "Someday you will throw yourself into the river, and I may not be here to pull you out."

What we all have to realize is that when we sin we turn our back on God. He does not turn His back on us. If we are ever to see His face again we must turn around, that is, turn from sin. That is what is meant by conversion. "Turn ye to me, saith the Lord of hosts" (Zechariah 1:3).

God cannot save us without that conversion; if we die in our unrepentant sin, we are forever turned away from God. Where the tree falleth there it lies. There is no reversal of values after death.

We cannot love sin during life and begin to love virtue at death. The joys of heaven are the continuance of the Christ-like joys of earth. We do not develop a new set of loves with our last breath. We shall reap in eternity only what we sowed on earth. If we loved sin, we shall reap corruption; but we shall never gather grapes from thistles.

The Justice of God is not separable from His Goodness. If He were not Just, He would not be Good. Because He is Goodness, His Justice pardons; because He is Justice, His Goodness expiates. The thief on the right saw the need of Justice the moment he admitted, "We suffer justly"; that is why immediately he felt the response of Goodness: "This Day . . . Paradise."

Then let not our presuming moderns who pile sin on sin think that they can insult God until their lease on life has run out and then expect an eternal lease on one of the Father's mansions. Did He who went to Heaven by a Cross intend that you should go there by sinning?

Let us consider the other type of soul: the despairing. As presumption forgets Divine Justice, so despair forgets Divine Mercy. Modern despair is not only hopeless about eternal life, which it doubts but even about earthly life, which it mocks. Never before in the history of Christianity has despair been so abysmal. Today there is everywhere an anticipation of catastrophe, an appalling sense of unpredictability and impending disaster.

In the past, men recovered from despair either by returning to the glories of the past or by looking forward to a crown beyond the cross; but now that minds have lost faith in God, they have only this world to give them hope.

Since that has turned against them, they feel a conscious rupture with hope. They curse a meaningless existence, succumb to a continuous exasperation with uncertainty, and yield to a suicidal intent to escape the inescapable.

There are two causes for modern despair: Sensuality and sadness. It is a fact that those poets who have most ridiculed the future life and those writers who have poured the most scorn on sin and Divine Justice were themselves most abandoned to sensuality.

The singers of voluptuousness are always the singers of despair. This is because sensuality produces continuous disillusionment. Its pleasures must be repeated because of their unsatisfyingness; therefore, they make hungry where most they satisfy.

Being deceived so many times by the alluring promises of the flesh, its addicts feel that all life is a deceit. Having been fooled by that which promised pleasure, they conclude that nothing can give pleasure. The fruit of pessimism blossom on the tree of a dissolute life.

From another point of view, sensuality begets despair because by its very nature it is directed to a sensual object, and an excessive dedication to the carnal kills the capacity for the spiritual. Delicate hands lose their skill by handling rough stones, and souls lose their appetite for the Divine by undue attachment to the flesh. The eyes that refuse to look upon the light soon lose their power to see: "Having eyes, [they] see . . . not" (Mark 8:18).

Hope implies love; but if love is centered in the corporal, the soul is deadened to all that is not carnal: It finds less and less satisfaction in duty, family, work, profession, and, above all else, God. There is time only for the wicked joy to which one is slave.

Naturally, the future life and heaven and the Cross cease to move such a person. There is no desire except the biological; the future begins to be disgusting. From a stage where there is no time for God, they reach another where there is no taste for God. Thus does a world, which forgot love for sex, pay its terrible penalty in the despair, which calls life meaningless because it has made its own life a wreck.

The second cause of despair is sadness. Sadness does not mean sorrow caused by a death, but rather a surrender to states of depression because of a consciousness of sin and unworthiness. Many falls produce melancholy; repeated defeats induce despair.

St. Paul speaks of carnal excesses and greed for money as the feeble compensations for the one who experiences melancholy induced by multiplied sin: "Who despairing have given themselves up to lasciviousness, unto the working of all uncleanness unto covetousness" (Ephesians 4:19).

Despair, born of the loss of God, also ends in persecution. In their impiety, such souls would kill the God they left. That is why wherever you find an atheistic government in the world today, you find "purges." Not being able to tolerate their own inner sadness, they must compensate for it by killing hope in others.

Each despairing soul must decide for itself the reason for despair. Regardless however of how multiplied or grievous your sins may have been, there is still room for hope. Did not Our Lord say: "For I came not to call the just, but sinners" (Mark 2:17); and on another occasion "there shall be joy in heaven upon one sinner that doth penance, more than upon ninety-nine just who need not penance" (Luke 15:7).

If He forgave the thief, and Magdalene, and Peter, why not you? What makes many in old age sad is not that their joys are gone, but that their hopes are gone. Your earthly hopes may decrease with the years, but not heavenly hope. Regardless of the sinful burden of the years, God's mercy is greater than your faults.

Only when God ceases to be infinitely merciful and only when you begin to be infinitely evil, will there be reason for despair; and that will be never; Peter denied Our Lord, but Our Lord did not deny Peter. The thief cursed Christ, but He did not curse the thief. If we had never sinned, we could never call Christ Saviour.

The Divine Invitation has never been annulled: "Come to me, all you that labour, and are burdened, and I will refresh you" (Matthew 11:28). That invitation is not only for the weary; it is also for the sinful.

If you insist that you are disgusted with yourself, remember that you can come to God even by a succession of disgusts. What does your disgust mean except that everything earthly has failed you? That is one of the ways God makes you feel hunger for the Divine. Do you not crave food most when you are hungry? Do you not want water most when you are thirsty?

Your own disgust, if you knew it, is the distant call of Divine Mercy. If then the poverty of your merits makes you shrink from the Divine Presence, then let your needs draw you to Him.

The principal reason for the increase of nervous disorders in the world is due to hidden guilt or unatoned sin locked on the inside until it festered. These souls are running off to psychoanalysts to have their sins explained away when what they need is to get down on their knees and right themselves with God.

When disgusted with our sins we can go into a confessional box, become our own accuser, hear the words of absolution Our Lord Himself gave, make amends and start life all over again, for none of us want our sins explained away; we want them forgiven. That is the miracle of the Sacrament of Penance and the rekindling of Hope.

"If I had sat at supper with the Lord
And laid my head upon that saving breast
I might have turned and fled among the rest –
I might have been that one who left the board
To add the high priests' silver to his hoard.
Had our Redeemer stooped to wash my feet,
Would I have washed my neighbor's clean and sweet
Or thrice denied the Christ I had adored?

"Long have I grieved that I was not St. Paul
Who rode those seas and saw the tempest toss
The ships he sailed in when he heard the call
To preach the risen Christ and gain through loss.
Tonight I envy most among them all
That thief who hung repentant on his cross."

Alexander Harvey

THE THIRD VIRTUE

- *Prudence* -

"Behold thy son; behold thy mother."

THE GREATEST CRISIS in the history of the world was the arrest and conviction of a Man found guilty of no other charge than an excess of love. What was tragic about that crisis reaching from a Garden to a Cross was: Man failed!

Peter, James, and John, who had been given the flashing light of the Transfiguration to prepare them for the dark night of Olives, slept as His enemies attacked. Judas, who had heard the Divine admonition to lay up treasures in Heaven, peddled his Master for thirty pieces of silver — for Divinity is always sold out of all proportion to due worth.

Peter who had been made the Rock and Key-bearer, warmed himself by a fire and with an atavistic throwback to his fisherman days, cursed and swore to a maidservant that he knew not the man.

As Pilate submitted to the crowd the choice of Christ or a revolutionary upstart, the mob chose Barabbas. Finally, on Calvary where were the men? Where were those whom He cured? Peter was not there, nor his brother Andrew, nor James, nor any of the other Apostles except John, who might not have been there had it not been for the encouragement given him by Mary.

But though men failed in this crisis, there is no instance of a single woman failing. In the four trials, the voice heard in His defense was that of a woman, Claudia Procul, the wife of Pontius Pilate, warning her husband not to do anything unjust to that just man. Events proved that the politician was wrong and the woman right.

On the way to Calvary, it is the woman who offers consolation, first Veronica wiping away the blood and sweat from His Sacred Face to receive the reward of Its imprint on her towel; then the holy women to whom the Prisoner turned suggesting that only such multiplied mercies and charities as their own could avert catastrophe for their children.

Again on Calvary, it is woman who is fearless, for there are several of them at the foot of the Cross. Magdalene, among them as usual, is prostrate. But there is one whose courage and devotion was so remarkable that the Evangelist who was there indicated the detail that she was "standing." That woman was the Mother of the Man on the Central Cross.

When we realize that He who is pinioned to that Cross is the Son of God and therefore possessed of Infinite Wisdom and Power, we are at first inclined to wonder why she should not have been spared the sorrow of Golgotha.

Since He had made her of incomparable beauty of body and soul, why should He not keep those eyes made for Paradise from gazing on a Cross? Why not shield ears attuned to the Divine Word from the blasphemies of ungrateful humans? Since preserved from original sin, why should its penalties be visited upon her? Must Mothers go to gallows with their sons? Must the innocent eat the bitter fruit planted by the sinful?

These are questions of false human wisdom, But God's ways are not our ways. Our Blessed Lord willed her presence there. Since He was the second Adam undoing the sin of the first, Mary would be the new Eve proclaiming the glory of womanhood in the new race of the redeemed.

The woman Eve would not be so cured that her most glorious daughter could not undo her evil. As a woman had shared in the fall of man, so woman should share in his redemption. In no better way could Our Lord reveal woman's role in the new order than by giving John, that disciple whom He loved above the others, to His Mother whom He loved above all: "Son! Behold thy Mother . . . Woman! Behold thy son! "

The Kingdom of God was born! Heavenly prudence had chosen the right means to reveal the new ties born of redemption. Mary was to be our Mother, and we her children.

The Saviour's death was at the same time a birth; the end of a chapter of crucifixion was the beginning of the chapter of a new creation.

As light is instantaneous in dispelling darkness so the Divine Saviour wills that not even a moment shall intervene between breaking down the attachments to Satan by sin and the incorporation of man into the Kingdom of God. She exchanges her Son for the advantages of the Passion and receives its first fruit — John. He had kept His word: "l will not leave you orphans" (John 14:18).

On the Cross was Wisdom Incarnate, dying that we might live. If Our Saviour could have thought of any better means of leading us back to Him, He would have put us in other hands than hers.

There are many falsehoods told about the Catholic Church: One of them is that Catholics adore Mary. This is absolutely untrue. Mary is a creature, human, not Divine. Catholics do not adore Mary. That would be idolatry. But they do reverence her.

And to those Christians who have forgotten Mary, may we ask if it is proper for them to forget her whom He remembered on the Cross? Will they bear no love for that woman through the portals of whose flesh, as the Gate of Heaven, He came to earth?

One of the reasons why so many Christians have lost a belief in the Divinity of Christ is because they lost all affection for her upon whose white body, as a Tower of Ivory, that Infant climbed "to kiss upon her lips a mystic rose."

There is not a Christian in all the world who reverences Mary who does not acknowledge Jesus her Son to be in Truth the Son of the Living God. The prudent Christ on the Cross knew the prudent way to preserve belief in His Divinity, for who better than a Mother knows her son?

The gift of Mary did something to man, for it gave him an ideal love. To fully appreciate this fact, dwell for a moment on the difference between two faculties: The intellect, which knows, and the will, which loves.

The intellect always whittles down the object to suit itself. That is why the intellect insists on examples, explanations, and analogies. Every teacher must accommodate himself to the mentality of his class, and if the problem, which he is presenting, is abstract and complicated, he must break it up into the concrete, as Our Lord described the mysteries of the Kingdom of God in parables.

But the will never works that way. While the intellect pulls down the object of knowledge to its level, the will always goes out to meet the object.

If you love something, you lift yourself up to its level; if you love music you subject yourself to its demands, and if you love mathematics you meet its conditions. We tend to become like that which we love. Boys who love gangsters are already the making of gangsters. As our loves are, that we are. We scale mountains if the object loved is on a mountain; we jump down into the abyss if the object loved is there.

It follows that the higher our loves and ideals, the nobler will be our character. The problem of character training is fundamentally the inculcation of proper ideals. That is why every nation holds up its national heroes, that citizens may become like to them in their patriotism and devotion to country.

If we have heroes and ideal prototypes for those who love sports, the stage, country, army, and navy, why should there not be an ideal in the all-important business of leading a good life and saving our souls?

That is precisely one of the roles the Blessed Mother of our Divine Lord plays in Christian life: An object of love so pure, so holy, and so motherly that to be worthy of it we refrain from doing anything which might offend her.

There has hardly ever been a mother in the history of the world who did not at one time or another say to her son or daughter: "Never do anything of which your mother would be ashamed." But what these mothers say is only an echo from the Cross, when Our Divine Lord gave us His Mother as our mother. In giving her to us, He was equivalently saying: "Never do anything of which your Heavenly Mother would be ashamed."

The nobler the love, the nobler the character, and what nobler love could be given to men than the woman whom the Saviour of the world chose as His own Mother?

Why is it that the world has confessed its inability to inculcate virtue in the young? Very simply because it has not co-related morality to any love nobler than self-love. Things keep their proportion and fulfill their proper role only when integrated into a larger whole.

Most lives are like doors without hinges, or sleeves without coats, or bows without violins; that is, unrelated to wholes or purposes which give them meaning.

If, for example, a speaker concentrates upon his hands, wonders whether he should put them in his pockets or behind his back, it will not be long until he feels he is all hands.

The modern emphasis on sex is a result of tearing a function away from a purpose, a part away from a whole. It can never be handled properly unless integrated to a larger pattern and made to serve it.

That is, to some extent, the role Our Blessed Mother plays in the moral life of our Catholic youth. She is that ideal love for which lesser and baser loves and impulses are sacrificed. Just as a skilled orator so integrates his hands into the pattern of speech that he is never conscious of their presence, so the Catholic youth maintains that healthy self-restraint out of respect for one whom he loves.

The level of any civilization is the level of its womanhood. What they are, men will be, for, to repeat, love always goes out to meet the demands of the object loved. Given a woman like the Mother of Our Lord as our supernatural Mother, you have one of the greatest inspirations for nobler living this world has ever known.

In this hour as never before the world needs to hear again this third word from the Cross. It needs the inspiration of the Good Woman. Unfortunately, the woman who is admired today is not the virtuous woman, but the beautiful woman — and by beautiful is meant not that inner beauty of the king's daughter, but that beauty which is only skin deep and sometimes only powder deep.

Glance at the advertisements flashed across the pages and billboards of our country! They are for the most part pictures of women who ten years from now would not be accepted for the same advertisement because they will have lost what they now possess — a passing beauty.

Our modern world does not really love woman; it loves only her external beauty. If it loved woman, it would love woman as long as she is woman. But because it loves the mask of a woman, it ignores the woman when the mask disappears.

The alarming increase of divorces in our land and the consequent break-up of family life is due principally to the loss of love for the ideal in womanhood. Marriage has become identified with pleasure, not with love. Once the pleasure ceases, love ceases. The woman is loved not for what she is in herself but for what she is to others. The tragedy of such a state is not only what it does for woman, but also what it does for man.

How restore love for woman as woman? By giving as the object of life's love a woman who has given Life and Love to the world — a Woman who is beautiful on the outside all the days of her life, because she is beautiful on the inside. That was the means Our Lord chose on the Cross to remake the world: Remake man by remaking the woman.

Conceived in the Divine Mind, sculptured by the creative fingers of the Heavenly Sculptor, touched by ever radiant color from the palette of heaven, the Artist on the Cross points to His masterpiece and says to man: "Behold the Woman!"

There is told a legend which illustrates the intercessory power of Our Blessed Lady: It seems that one day Our Blessed Lord was walking through the Kingdom of Heaven and saw some souls who had got in very easily. Approaching Peter at the Golden Gate, He said: "Peter, I have given to you the keys to the Kingdom of Heaven. You must use your power wisely and discreetly. Tell Me, Peter, how did these souls gain entry into My Kingdom?" To which Peter answered: "Don't blame me, Lord. Every time I close the door, Your Mother opens a window."

When amidst the thousand and one allurements of this world you know not which way to turn, pray to the Woman — the Virgin most prudent. She knows the true from the false, for in the language of Joyce Kilmer:

At the foot of the Cross on Calvary
Three soldiers sat and diced
And one of them was the devil
And he won the Robe of Christ.

I saw him through a thousand veils
And has not this sufficed?
Now, must I look on the devil robed
In the radiant robe of Christ?

He comes, his face is sad and mild
With thorns, his head is crowned
There are great bleeding wounds in His feet
And in each hand a wound.

How can I tell, who am a fool
If this be Christ or no?
Those bleeding hands outstretched to me
Those eyes that love me so!

I see the robe – I look, I hope
I fear – but there is one
Who will direct my troubled mind.
Christ's Mother knows her Son.

O Mother of Good Counsel, lend
Intelligence to me
Encompass me with wisdom
Thou Tower of Ivory!

"This is the man of lies" she says
"Disguised with fearful art:
He has the wounded hands and feet
But not the wounded heart."

Beside the Cross on Calvary
She watched them as they diced
She saw the devil join the game
And win the Robe of Christ.

"The Robe of Christ"
MAIN STREET AND OTHER POEMS
*by **Joyce Kilmer***
©1917 Doubleday, Doran & Company Inc.

THE FOURTH VIRTUE

- *Faith* -

"My God! My God!
Why hast thou forsaken me?"

HOW MANY WHO profess no formal religion could tell what they disbelieve? The question is put that way because years ago many who did not have faith knew what they disbelieved and why; today those who do not have faith do not even know what they disbelieve. Having abandoned all certitudes, they have no standards by which to judge even their own agnosticism.

And now, with the depression, war, and its consequent insecurity, they have begun to doubt their own doubts. The words 'progress' 'evolution' and 'science' which once thrilled them and gave them the illusion of faith, now leave them cold.

Many today feel that their life is discontinuous; that each act of their will is unrelated to any other; that their bad actions of the past, like a spent arrow, are gone and forgotten; that their life because ephemeral is unrelated to any responsibility, and that their last week's self is no longer their worry, nor what they will be next week their moral concern.

Their life is like a Japanese lantern, made up of thousands of designs, but without unity. They may know much, but they cannot put their fields of learning into a unity.

Their knowledge is like the shelves in a drug store, filled with bottles of wisdom one unrelated to another, but not like a living thing in which organs, cells, and functions flow into a unity of purpose.

What they need to do is put a candle inside the Japanese lantern of their life: or a soul into their discontinuous chemical existence in order to recover the meaning of life, and that candle and that soul is faith.

Faith is not, as too many believe, an emotional trust; it is not a belief that something will happen to you; it is not even a will to believe despite difficulties. Rather faith is the acceptance of a truth on the authority of God revealing. It, therefore, presupposes reason. What credit is to business that faith is to religion.

Before extending you credit, the businessman must have a reason for extending that credit, namely, your ability to pay debts and your honesty. So it is with faith. You cannot start religion with faith, for to believe someone without a reason for belief is credulity and superstition.

The principal cause for the decline of religion in America is the irrational and groundless character of belief. Unless the foundation is solid the superstructure soon totters and falls. Try out the experiment and ask those who call themselves Christians why they believe and the majority of them will be found unable to give a reason.

When anyone asks us to join the Church, he is not immediately accepted. He must first undergo instructions of between forty and one hundred hours extending over several months. Converts are not first told: "You must believe everything the Catholic Church teaches" but rather "You must have a reason for believing its teachings." Absolutely nothing is taken for granted. We do not say: "We will start with God." No! We start with the world. Using reason we, first prove the existence of God and His nature.

Enquiry precedes conviction. Enquiry is a matter for reason which weighs the evidence and says: "I ought to believe." But submission is an act of the will. It is at this point many fail, either because too absorbed by the pleasures of the world, or because fearful of the scorn of others.

But once it is admitted, thanks to the illumining grace of God, that Christ is the Son of God; there can be no picking and choosing among the parts of His Gospel.

Since Truth is life, it must like a living babe, be accepted in its entirety. Just as we are not falsely broadminded about life and accept a child on condition he has no arms or only one eye, so neither can we say we will believe Christ when He talks about lilies of the field and not believe Him when He talks about the sanctity of the family. It is all or nothing. "He that gathereth not . . . scattereth" (Matthew 12:30).

That is why the condition of becoming a Catholic is the total, complete and absolute submission to the authority of Christ and its prolongation in the Church. A Catholic may be defined as one who made the startling discovery that God knows more than he does.

Faith is related to reason as a telescope to the eye, which does not destroy vision, but opens new worlds hitherto closed to it. We have the same eyes at night as we have in the day, but we cannot see at night because we lack normally the additional light of the sun.

Let two minds with exactly the same education, one without and the other with faith, look on a piece of unleavened bread in a monstrance. The one sees bread; the other adores the Eucharistic Lord. One sees more than the other because he has a light which the other lacks — the light of faith.

For some illustrations of the virtue of faith, we look in particular to the Fourth Word spoken from the pulpit of the Cross.

For almost three hours Our Lord hung upon the Cross, while the sun wore the crêpe of darkness in mourning for the Light of the World. Men might look on the sad spectacle of a Crucified Lord, but the sun could not endure it and hid its face.

The Evangelists record the Fourth Word as being spoken when darkness covered the earth, which means that it was as night, not only in nature but in the heart and soul of Jesus. It was a moment of mysterious voluntary surrender of Divine consolation, a second of seeming God-forsakenness.

Man had already abandoned Him. They chose Barabbas to Him; they even begrudged Him enough of their earth to stretch out and die as they lifted Him above it on a tree.

Now God seems to abandon Him, as in the midst of the stygian blackness at high noon He spoke this time in Hebrew, the language of the Prophet and the Psalm. The tones were loud and clear: "Eli, Eli, lamma sabacthani" — "My God, my God, why hast thou forsaken me?" (Matthew 27:46).

During His life some of His disciples left Him and walked with Him no more; only the night before at the Last Supper He said: "Behold, the hour cometh, and it is now come, that you shall be scattered every man to his own, and shall leave me alone..." (John 16:32).

That hour was upon Him now. He refused to be spared what His adopted brethren must share. He was "made sin" for us by taking upon Himself the condition which sin merited. What did sin merit? Abandonment by God.

Creatures turned against the Creator; the sheep rebelled against the Shepherd, the pilgrims left the fountains of living waters and dug for themselves broken cisterns that could hold no water. He willed to experience that isolation and abandonment. Hence the words: "Why hast thou forsaken me?"

And yet it was not total abandonment for it was prefaced by God: "My God, my God!" The sun does not abandon its task to light a world because temporarily overshadowed by a cloud. Because these misty shapes hide its light and heat, we still know a day of dawning is near.

Furthermore, the Fourth Word was a verse from a Psalm of faith which ends: "He hath not slighted nor despised the supplication of the poor man. Neither hath he turned away his face from me: and when I cried to him, he heard me" (Psalm 21:25).

In the perspective of this Word of Faith there are these three practical conclusions:

1) The object of faith is God, not the things of earth. Too many interpret faith as that which should release us from the ills of earth and assume that if we do suffer it is because we lack faith. This is quite untrue. Faith in God is no assurance that we will be spared the "arrows of outrageous fortune."

He was not. Why should we? It was His enemies who thought that if He were one with God, He should not suffer, for when He said: "Eli, Eli" they, imagining He called for Elias, sneered: "See whether Elias will come to deliver him" (Matthew 27:49). Because He was not delivered, they concluded He must be wicked. No! Faith does not mean being taken down from a cross; it means be lifted up to heaven — sometimes by a cross.

The only times some people think of God is when they are in trouble, or when their pocketbook is empty, or they have a chance to make it a little fatter. They flatter themselves that at such moments they have faith when really they have only earthly hope for good luck.

It cannot be repeated too often: faith bears on the soul and its salvation in God, not on the baubles of earth.

2) Scripture states that when they crucified Christ, darkness covered the earth. That is exactly the description of our modern world. If the darkness of despair, the black-outs of peace make our world wander blindly, it is because we have crucified the Light of the World.

Witness within the last twenty years how religion has been nailed to the Cross in Russia, scourged in Germany, crowned with thorns in Spain, martyred in Poland, and lashed in Mexico.

No wonder our statesmen know not which way to turn: they are either putting out or permitting to be put out the only Light which illumines the pathways of justice and peace.

It may be that our woes are the last stage of sin. For a century or more governments and people have abandoned God; now God is abandoning them. It is a terrible punishment when a just God strikes, but it is more terrible when He does not but leaves us alone to our own devices to work out the full consequences of our sins.

We are at the end of a tradition and a civilization which believes we could preserve

Christianity without Christ: religion without a creed, meditation without sacrifice, family life without moral responsibility, sex without purity, and economics without ethics.

We have completed our experiment of living without God and have proven the fallacy of a system of education which calls itself progressive because it finds new excuses for sins.

Our so-called progressiveness did we but realize it, is like unto the progressive putrefaction of a corpse. The soul is gone, and what we call change is only decay.

There is no stopping it except by reversing the process by which we drove God out of the world, namely by relighting the lamp of faith in the souls of men.

3) Here is a common burden of all believers in God. There is, unfortunately, a far greater unity among the enemies of God than among His friends. On the one hand, we have the spectacle of Hitler and Stalin burying their mutual hatreds because they found a greater hatred — God and religion.

On the other hand, what are we believers in God doing to preserve religion, morality, and culture? Too often we wage a civil war, attacking one another, while a common enemy storms our altars. This does not mean we must abandon creeds, and water down the milk of religion to a point where it would no longer nourish.

The Catholic Church for one would never do that because since its truths are God-made, they cannot be man-unmade. We are trustees not creators of faith.

But we do recognize that with Protestants and Jews we have God, morality, and religion in common. In the name of God, let us, Jews, Protestants and Catholics, do two things: 1) Realize that an attack upon one is an attack upon all since we are all one in God; it is not Tolerance we need, but Charity; not forbearance but love.

3) Begin doing something about religion and the least we can do is to say our prayers: to implore God's blessings upon the world and our country; to thank Him for His blessings, and to become illumined in the fullness of His truth. There is entirely too much talk about religion and not enough action.

If we followed the same rules for health that we do about religion, we would all be bedridden. It is not enough to talk about the necessity of health; we must do something practical about it, for example, eat, exercise and rest.

So it is with religion. We must nourish ourselves with the truths of God, exercise our spiritual muscles in prayer, mortify ourselves of those things which are harmful to the soul, and be just as scrupulous in avoiding moral evil as we are in avoiding physical evil.

Faith being a virtue is a habit, — not an acquired habit like swimming, but an infused habit given to us by God in Baptism. Being a habit, it grows by practice.

The ideal is to reach a point in practice, where, like unto Our Lord on the Cross, we witness to God even amidst abandonment and the agony of a crucifixion.

THE FIFTH VIRTUE

- *Temperance* -

"I Thirst."

THERE IS A WORLD of difference between what we need and what we want. We need those things which are essential for a normal, comfortable human existence; but we want more than that. Our needs are quickly satisfied, but our wants rarely.

The day our Blessed Lord multiplied the loaves and fishes the Evangelist records that each person had his fill and was satisfied. But just suppose that Our Lord instead of giving food which they needed, miraculously multiplied money and gave each of them the equivalent of a ten-dollar bill. How many, do you think, would have been satisfied with one bill? Money is a want; food is a need.

Because our needs are limited, but our wants are unlimited, a virtue is necessary to restrain our inordinate appetites and desires — and that virtue is called temperance. It has for its object the regulation of the sensible appetites by reason.

The two strongest appetites in man are eating and drinking which sustain his individual life and the sexual act which propagates his social nature. Excesses in these appetites are the sources of the two sins of gluttony and lust. Temperance is the virtue which moderates them for the sake of the soul.

Temperance must not be confused either with Puritanism, which because of the abuse of a thing would take away its use; or with license, which would interpret all restraint as an infringement of liberty. Rather, there is a golden mean, as revealed in Our Lord's first miracle at Cana, where He changed water into wine to satisfy the individual appetite and blessed the married couple for the satisfaction of the creative instinct.

There is no consolation here for those gloomy souls who would kill the joy of living, nor for those frivolous souls who would isolate pleasure from the end of living, namely, the salvation of the soul.

Temperance reaches its peak in Him who came to preach the hard way of the cross and yet began it by serving wine and assisting at a marriage feast. For that reason, the extremists who want all fast or all feast were never pleased with His Temperance.

As He said to them on one occasion: "For John came neither eating nor drinking; and they say: He hath a devil. The Son of man came eating and drinking, and they say: Behold a man that is a glutton and a wine drinker a friend of publicans and sinners" (Matthew 11:18-19). It is so hard to please those who are looking for faults.

Finally, on the Cross, He gave us His Fifth Word — the revelation of the philosophy of temperance. Racked by the burning fever of crucifixion, like a dying soldier on a battlefield His lips craved for water. There was a physical foundation of the cry: "I thirst" (John 19:28).

But it looked to something else. St. John who was at the foot of the Cross records that He said it "that the scriptures might be fulfilled" (John 19:28).

A thousand years before the Psalmist had prophesied that hour: "And they gave me gall for my food, and in my thirst, they gave me vinegar to drink" (Psalm 68:22).

The cry was not a cry of weakness, nor selfishness, but a proclamation that the material exists for the spiritual; the appetites and thirsts of earth must be the stepping stones to the hunger and thirst for the kingdom of God and His Justice.

From this Word we learn two lessons of Temperance: First, the material exists for the spiritual. Christ expressed a physical thirst for a spiritual reason, namely, the fulfillment of prophecy as a proof of His divinity. In like manner, every material thing on the face of this earth, from salt to flesh, must be for us, a means, not an end — a bridge, not a goal of life.

A glutton does not respect this order; he does not eat to live but lives to eat. He subordinates life to one of its conditions. The glutton or the drunkard is really a person without a sense of humor. He takes food and drink too seriously; he always misses the reference.

He takes drink so seriously that he forgets it was meant to assist locomotion, not to impede it; he takes flesh so seriously that he forgets it was meant to solder life, not to scorch it.

Why are there so many unhappy marriages today? Because instead of marrying for the reason that human love is the vestibule to the Divine, they marry wondering how long they will be married. On the way back from the Justice of the Peace they are already preparing for divorce as one says to the other: "I will love you for two years and six months."

There was once a time when a man who married a woman would no more have thought of divorcing her than of murdering her. But those were the days when men loved because they believed in God; now they lust because they believe in Freud — for if this world is all there is, then why not get all you can and by whatever means you can.

It is only in the Church today that "life without lust is born," because she teaches that the use of flesh conditions salvation. But in our modern divorce-mad world "lust without life shall die."

Because temperance teaches us that the earthly exists for the heavenly, the motive of a Christian is far different from the motive of a pagan.

Take two persons who by cutting down on their food lose twenty pounds each. Materially, twenty pounds off a pagan is the same as twenty pounds off a Christian. But the motive in each case is quite different. The pagan diets; the Christian fasts. The pagan diets for the sake of his bodily appearance; the Christian fasts for the sake of his soul. Each received his corresponding reward, either the praise of men who love leanness or the praise of God who loves virtue.

The tragedy of so much dieting, from a Catholic point of view, is how much restraint, or shall we say fat, that goes to waste. That is why one of the first questions in our Catechism is: "Of which should we take more care, our soul or our body?" And the answer is: "We should take more care of our soul, for 'what doth it profit a man if he gain the whole world, and suffer the loss of his immortal soul?'"

It is the rigid adherence to this principle that the material exists for the spiritual, which makes the Catholic school one of the greatest training grounds for character in the world. Little children are taught as soon as they enter school to 'give up' certain things during Lent — not because candy is bad, but in order that they might be self-controlled and self-possessed. It is the contrary to the pagan philosophy of 'self-expression' or doing whatever you please.

A boiler that refuses to keep within the limits and blows up is self-expressive. A drunkard is self-expressive or liquor-possessed because he is not self-possessed. Liquor is not his servant; he is its slave. We Catholics do not eat meat on Friday because we love our Lord. That is the day on which He died, and out of loving memory for this redemption we give up the pleasure of meat — and most of us Catholics hate fish — because He gave up His life for us. Is that anything to be scorned?

The basis of the Catholic secret of temperance and discipline is exchange. All life is founded on exchange: "What exchange shall a man give?" We get light in exchange for heat; bread in exchange for a dime. If you want to be an expert in mathematics you have to give up being an expert in tennis; if you want to give your body all its satisfactions, you have to give up the joys of the soul. We have to pay for everything.

Every joy demands that another be left untouched. Every step forward requires an austerity, but that is not because there are no rewards on the other side of the hill, but only because we cannot see what is on the other side of the hill.

We must choose then between God and Mammon; flesh and spirit. "No man can serve two masters." If we want to save our soul for eternity, we must discipline our body in time. And we do this not with sadness but with gladness, after the example of Him "who having joy set before him endured the Cross."

A saint is always joyful, but our modern pleasure-hunter is always melancholy. He is not really happy because he laughs too much. His laughter is artificially stimulated from the outside by a stooge with a wise-crack; it is not a joy that proceeds from the inside because of a duty fulfilled out of love of God. Happiness comes from self-possession through temperance, not from self-expression through license.

The second lesson of temperance in this Fifth Word is given us by the soldier who shared his wine with Our Lord. The cry of Our Lord was not addressed to anyone in particular, but as others wondered what to do, he did it. Scripture says "he ran."

There was no irresoluteness about his service; only one thought dominated his mind: "His need is greater than mine." The Gospel notes that he filled the sponge. It was unusual for an executioner to share rations with the one to be executed, but there was something very un-criminal about that man on the central cross.

The wine he gave was not much, but God considers not the gift of the giver, but the love of the giver. The soldier could not reach the lips of Our Lord, so he placed the sponge on a reed and touched it to the lips of the Saviour. He had shared his wine with his Creator, and if he knew it, also with his Saviour. And until the crack of doom, his act like that of Magdalene shall be recorded among men.

As he restrained himself in the use of his lawful possessions out of love of the suffering, so must we share our treasures out of love for the poor. Here again, the motive of sharing is more important than the deed. The reward we will get for our giving depends on the intention of our giving.

We love those who love us — but there is no great reward in this, for "do not the heathens this." But we must love even our enemies that we may be children of Our Father who is in heaven. Loving enemies out of a divine intention is worth more than loving friends out of a personal satisfaction.

The philanthropists who give millions to erect art museums, libraries, and playgrounds out of purely humanitarian reasons, will not further their eternal salvation as much as the poor widow who gives a nickel to a poor man on the street because in his need she sees the poverty of Christ. It is simply a matter of bookkeeping.

Suppose you wanted to establish a credit for purchases. Naturally, if you deposited your money on credit in a furniture store, you could not expect it to be honored at an automobile factory. In like manner, if you give lavishly to be credited by mankind, you cannot expect to be credited by Christ for eternal salvation. Millions given to perpetuate a family name will avail the soul nothing at the moment of judgment.

This does not mean that money given for art institutes and playgrounds do not avail for eternal salvation, but that they avail only on condition they were given for that motive, that is, in His name: "For whosoever shall give you to drink a cup of water in my name, because you belong to Christ: Amen I say to you, he shall not love his reward" (Mark 9:40).

St. Paul, emphasizing that charity or the love of God alone makes deeds profitable unto salvation, is even more emphatic: "If I should distribute all my goods to feed the poor, and if I should deliver my body to be burned, and have not charity, it profiteth me nothing" (1 Corinthians 13:3).

There is a story told of a woman who gave a fortune motivated by human glory, and very occasionally a meager gift for a spiritual intention. When she went to heaven St. Peter showed her a tiny insignificant little house, which was dwarfed by all the mansions surrounding it. "I cannot live in that," said the woman. St. Peter answered: "Sorry, lady. That was the best I could do with the materials you sent me."

It is one of the paradoxes of Christianity that the only things that are really our own when we die is what we gave away in His name. What we leave in our wills is snatched from us by death; but what we give away is recorded by God to our eternal credit, for only our works follow us. It is not what is given that profits unto salvation; it is why it is given.

That is why a friendly meal given to an enemy in the name of Him Who loved us when we were His enemies, is worth more on the day of our judgment than a ten-million-dollar hospital given to perpetuate a family name.

There is no injustice in this. Each gets the reward he wanted: In one instance, the love of Christ; in the other the memory of men. Of the latter, Our Lord said the saddest words ever spoken: "They already have their reward."

For those who wish to cultivate the virtue of temperance and to be self-possessed, these two specific recommendations are made: First, each day practice at least three trivial mortifications, for example, giving up the ninth cigarette, holding back the sarcastic word, returning a kindly answer to a sneer, or sealing the lips on the scandal you just heard, which probably, like all scandals, is 99 44/100 percent untrue.

Second, the magnitude of the mortification is not as important as the love of God for which it is done. Great sacrifices without love are worthless for the soul; nor because they are great does it follow they were done with love; it is the motive that matters — do them out of love of God.

Then amid the crosses and trials of life, you may catch their relation to the Cross, which alone gives a pattern to the contradiction of life. May we all, like unto the soldier, Joyce Kilmer, as he trudged across the fields of France, see in every aching shoulder, feverish brow, and burning hand, the vision of Christ with His Cross:

My shoulders ache beneath my pack
(Lie easier, Cross, upon His back).

I march with feet that burn and smart
(Tread, Holy Feet, upon my heart).

Men shout at me who may not speak
(They scourged Thy back and smote Thy cheek).

I may not lift a hand to clear
My eyes of salty drops that sear.

(Then shall my fickle soul forget
Thy Agony of Bloody Sweat?)

My rifle hand is stiff and numb
(From Thy pierced palm red rivers come).

Lord, Thou didst suffer more for me
Than all the hosts of land and sea.

So let me render back again
This millionth of Thy gifts.   Amen.

POEMS, ESSAYS AND LETTERS
by **Joyce Kilmer**
©*1914, 1918 Doubleday, Doran and*
Company Inc.

THE SEVEN VIRTUES

THE SIXTH VIRTUE

- *Justice* -

"It is consummated."

CALVARY IS NOT A HISTORY everyone likes to hear recalled, and generally, those who most shrink from the sight of the Saviour on the Cross are the very ones who delight in the grotesque murder stories in our tabloids and follow with bold interest the harrowing details of a sex crime.

Why is it that the lover of horror cannot stand the sight of the crucifix? Why is it that the fanatics of murder stories are so cold to the story of the world's greatest sacrifice? The answer is that unlike all other crimes the crucifix is self-accusing.

We can look on other scenes of injustice without feeling we are involved in them; but we cannot look on a crucifix without feeling that we had something to do with it, either for better or worse; either as a robber brought before his victim for judgment, or as a drowning man brought before his rescuer for thanks.

In the face of all things else, we can remain somewhat indifferent, for inhuman injustice the issues of right and wrong are not always clear-cut. But on Calvary there is an absoluteness; there are no streaks of grey, no blurred edges, only a straight collision of black and white, of good and evil — and there is no 'No Man's Land' between them.

It is the epitome of the struggle of the world; we are involved in it to the extent that we are involved in the conflict of good and evil. It would be convenient at times if we could wash our hands of the whole affair as Pilate tried to do; but deeper than the blood on Lady Macbeth's hands, not all the waters of the seven seas could wash away those spots incarnadined.

In the Crucifix is symbolized the perennial crisis in the soul of every man, the choice between the illusory end of time and the imponderable ends of eternity. First are focused all the microscopic conflicts of good and evil that go on in every conscience; or, to put it another way, every man's soul is Calvary written small. That is why the Crucifix is inescapable; we either shrink from it, or we embrace it, but we cannot be indifferent to it. Slinking away from it like a frightened animal is only the dishonest way of saying it is 'self-accusing.'

It is part of that perverse psychology which makes us suit our thinking to the way we live, rather than suiting the way we live to our thinking. There are really only two classes of souls in all the world: those who have the courage to contemplate the Crucifix and the cowards who run from it.

For those who are brave enough to look at the Crucifix, there is a revelation of the moral order — not a moral order based on abstractions, theories, and hypotheses, but a moral order revealed in a Person of absolute goodness who has met the impact of human evil.

It is more like a mirror than a scene, for it reveals not something unrelated to us, but ourselves, our moral beggary, our perversities, and our defeats.

Like nothing else in all the world, it seems to ask the questions: "Where do you stand?" "Which side do you propose to take from this moment on — My side, or the side of moneyed Judas, cowardly Pilate, crafty Annas, or lustful Herod?" We cannot escape an answer.

If on that Cross were someone who himself had been wrong and failed and had compromised with goodness, we could plead an excuse. But here neutrality is impossible because there is no question of something more good or less good — there is only right and wrong.

No answer is the wrong answer. By the answer we give, we judge ourselves. We cannot be on both sides, any more than we can be in Light and Darkness at the same time.

No wonder so many dislike the sight of a Crucifix; no wonder they hate their consciences; no wonder they try to drown its warnings in noise and excitement; no wonder they change the subject of conversation when anyone mentions death, or sneer when they are reminded of sin.

The Cross they can look at, for that might be only a symbol of the contradictions of life; but the Crucifix — they call it 'horrible' when they mean it is accusing.

They may run away from it during life, but they will meet it at the Eternal Judgment, when the Son of Man shall come bearing the Cross in triumph in the clouds of heaven, to render to every man according to his works.

The modern mood of mutilating the Gospel, choosing some texts, and ignoring others, makes men miss the purpose of the life of Christ. He came on earth not primarily to preach, but to redeem. He came less to live than to die.

His mission was not one of mere benevolence, nor to create a revolution in politics or economics, nor to heal, nor to leave a humanitarian ethics — all were these secondary to the one absorbing purpose of His life, the redemption of man.

The sublime declaration of His coming is set down by St. John: "God so loved the world, as to give his only begotten Son; that whosoever believeth in him, may not perish, but may have life everlasting" (John 3:16). Those who regard Christ as no more than a teacher cannot explain either His death or the desire for it.

If a fisherman sitting calmly on a dock throws himself into the sea to prove that he loves his neighbor who is calmly seated beside him, the act is meaningless. But if his neighbor actually fell in and the fisherman jumped into the sea to give up his life to save him, then we should say: "Greater love than this no man hath" (John 15:13).

In like manner, the plunging of Christ into the sea of human suffering is explicable only on the assumption that we were in danger of being drowned by sin. He came to pay a debt and by His obedience in the flesh to expiate our disobedience, and form to Himself a new race of men: He by whom the world was made (Philippians 2: 8-11).

What often happens in the economic order, happened in the moral order; man contracted a bigger debt than he could pay. A sin against Divine Love is greater than man alone can repair.

But if God undertook to forgive the debt through mercy, justice would have been unrequited. God, of course, could pay the debt of man's sin, but He could not in justice; do it apart from man.

A judge will not permit a stranger to walk off the street into a courtroom and take the death sentence of a murderer. In like manner, God could not pay our debt unless He became in some way involved in it.

This the Son of God, Jesus Christ, did by becoming man, assuming a human nature like unto us in all things save sin. He did not merely substitute for us, nor take our place; there is an identification of Him with us. He is the Head of our sin-laden race. In a certain sense, He and we are one Person — the new Adam.

Strictly speaking, Our Lord is man in an absolute sense, not just a man; His humiliation was not so much in assuming a human nature, but in making Himself one with us in the sinful conditions which we created.

He came not into an ideal world, but into this world of sin and suffering — not as a stranger to this life and lot, but as one bearing the burden of the world's sin in Himself, though Himself sinless. He submitted to put on the form and habit of man and to prove His obedience to the Divine Will in the face of temptation, as you and I must do it.

He willed to become the target of the hatred and scorn and mockery of God, and the effect of it was awful, for He faced sin in both its accumulated and massed power and in its experiential delights.

He humbled Himself in taking upon Himself the temporal penal consequences, which are the result of the moral disorder which sin wrought. By His submission to them for our sake He made in Himself the expiation for our sinful nature, becoming, as it were, the living crucible in which the dross of our sinful lives is burned away, that we might be once again pure gold consecrated to God's holy purposes.

It was not that our sins were transferred to Him that we might be guiltless, but that by accepting allegiance with our human nature, He willed to be visited upon Him the conditions which our sins deserved.

Not as a mere man bearing a limited share of the world's burden for sin did He suffer, but as the God-Man whose human suffering embraced within itself the uttermost suffering which sin can bring — physical and mental pain consequent on human mortality; utter self-abnegation for the pride and avarice of men; and defenseless crucifixion for the world's arrogance and brute force.

Thus did He will that in Him our suffering might be transmuted from penalty into expiation, and be the beginning of a new life in Him.

That is why when the hour comes for Him freely to lay down His life; He offers no defense. As a guilty person, He stands before the Judges; silently He listens to the charges and the condemnation; all forces of evil are allowed their free play.

Finally, the Cross was not merely the outbreak of human passion — it was the violent expression of anti-God. It was sin in its essence — the attempted destruction of Divinity.

Sin is self-mutilation, the destruction of personality — when it takes the form of pride, it crowns Goodness with thorns; when it takes the form of dishonesty, it nails hands to a Cross; when it takes the form of hate, it blasphemes the dying; when it takes the form of lust, it crucifies.

Nothing less than bloodshed could have been sin's worst crime and registered sin's deepest hurt.

Evil must work its power to the bitter end, use all its hatred, exhaust all its deceits, unsheathe all of its bloody swords, that being exhausted, Goodness may be revealed as triumphant.

And now that evil was spent in the final act of crucifixion, seeing that in Justice the last farthing was paid in the red coin of His blood and the mortgage against man paid back, He uttered His Cry of Triumph: "It is consummated."

All history, pagan and Jewish, looked forward to this moment; Heaven and earth were separated — now they could be united.

The Pontiff or Bridge-builder has spanned the shores of eternity and time, and the Bridge is the Cross. The last rivet has been put in place; the last nail driven . . . It is consummated.

This is the meaning of a Crucifix: His death is not necessitated by the perverse will of sinful men, and, therefore, is not a martyrdom; but rather a willing submission to their perverse will in order to awaken men to the malignity of their sin and thereby win them over to repentance.

In this one and the same act there stands revealed the awful malignity of sin and the Goodness of God, for it is the Victim who forgives. It was the beauty and loveliness of the God-Man Christ which on the one hand made the crime so great, and on the other hand, made the Divine forgiveness so final and so certain.

That Figure on the Cross bore to the full not only the physical effects of sin which any man might suffer, and not only the mental effects of sin which all of us ought to feel, but the spiritual effects of sin which only He could feel because being sinless, He was not part of it. Only the sinless know the horror of sin.

If you can stand the gaze of a Crucifix long enough, you will discover these truths. First, if sin cost Him, Who is Innocence, so much, then I who am guilty cannot take it lightly; second, there is only one thing worse in all the world than sin — and that is to forget I am a sinner; third, more bitter than the Crucifixion must be my rejection of that Love by which I was redeemed.

Every law, physical or moral, has its penalties. If I disobey the law of health, nature penalizes me with sickness. If I disobey the moral law, I cannot eternally hope to escape its consequences as though I had not violated it.

Some time may intervene between the sowing and the harvest, the wheat and the cockle may be permitted to grow together; but there one day comes the day of judgment when the wheat is gathered into barns, and the cockle is burned.

Suppose now you admitted that you were a sinner, and you wished to be justified by that Redemption. How would you put the two together? How would you tie up a sinful heart with that Cross? How span 1900 years to make Redemption effective in you — now at this hour? This is a very practical question and merits an answer.

It would be easy to answer if that Cross could be lifted out of the rocks of Calvary by some giant hand and set down in the very midst of our cities and in the center of our plains.

Suppose such a miracle actually happened, so that instead of looking back in memory and imagination to Calvary as something that happened we could see Calvary re-enacted before our very eyes, so truly and really that we could gain the same merit as if we stood on Good Friday beneath the shadow of the Cross.

Suppose in some visible way we could "show the death of the Lord until he come" (1 Corinthians 11:26), that we might incorporate ourselves to it as Mary and John did on Calvary.

We have a right to expect that the Memorial of His Passion be prolonged to this hour, for did He not give that Memorial the night before He died by consecrating bread and wine into His own body and blood, and tell His Apostles to do it in memory of Him?

If that Redemptive Death could be so visibly re-enacted in our days of war and woe and misery, then the Cross would not be a memory, but an action; not a prayer but a renewed sacrifice; not a thing unrelated to us, but something made available for our participation.

It almost sounds too good to be true. But that is precisely what has happened! For Catholics, the Mass is Calvary renewed! On the Cross He was alone; in the Mass, we are with Him. In that sense, Christ is still on the Cross.

THE SEVENTH VIRTUE

- Charity -

"Father, into thy hands I commend my spirit."

CHARITY IS THE PERFECTION of Justice. As Aristotle put it so wisely: "Where Justice is, there is a further need of friendship; but where friendship is, there is no need of justice." Complementing that last thought, St. Augustine said: "Love God and do whatever you please," for if you love God, you will never do anything to offend Him.

It was, therefore, fitting that the Sixth Word, reflecting the Justice of God which fulfilled the will of the Father in its smallest detail, should be followed by the Seventh Word of Charity: "Father, into Thy Hands I commend My Spirit." It was like the seventh day of Creation. During the six words, the Son of God labored forgiving enemies, pardoning thieves, solacing a mother, atoning for faithlessness, pleading for love, atoning for injustice, and now He takes His rest and goes back home.

Love is to a great extent a stranger on earth; it finds momentary satisfactions in human hearts, but it soon becomes restless. It was born of the Infinite and can never be satisfied with anything less. In a certain sense, God spoiled us for any other love except Himself, because He made us out of His Divine Love.

Born of His Everlasting Fire, the earthly sparks of affection can but kindle our hearts. We are all kings in exile; prodigals from the Father's House. As flames must mount upward to the sun, so He Who came from the Father must go back again to the Father: Love must return to Love. "Father, into Thy Hands I commend My Spirit."

It is noteworthy that He said these words with a loud voice. No one was taking His life away. It was not like the love expressed by a dying parent to his child; such love is begotten of a heart meeting the impact of the inevitable. But in the case of Our Lord, it was completely and absolutely unforced — the deliverance of freedom.

Thus did He teach us that all love on this earth involves choice. When, for example, a young man expresses his love to a young woman and asks her to become his wife, he is not just making an affirmation of love; he is also negating his love for anyone else. In that one act by which he chooses her, he rejects all that is not her.

There is no other real way in which to prove we love a thing than by choosing it in preference to something else. Words and sighs of love may be, and often are, expressions of egotism or passion; but deeds are proofs of love.

When God put Adam and Eve in the garden, the preservation of their gifts was conditioned upon fidelity to Him. But how prove fidelity except by choice, namely by obeying God's Will in preference to any other will.

In the freedom of choosing a fruit to a garden, was hidden the test of their love. By their decision, they proved they loved something else more than God.

After the Resurrection, Our Lord prefaced the conferring of the powers of jurisdiction on Peter as the Rock of the Church, by asking the question: "Simon, Son of John, lovest thou Me more than these?" Three times the question is asked because three times Peter had denied Our Lord — Once again, love is tested by preference.

The beginning and the end of the public life of Our Lord reveals this same basic quality of love. On the Mount of Temptation and on the Mount of Calvary, Satan and wicked men throw bribes into the balance to influence His choice. Surveying all the grandeur of earth, Satan in a frightening boast said: "All these kingdoms are mine." He offered them all to Our Lord if falling down He would adore him. Jesus could have the world if He would give up heaven.

Now on the other mount, it is satanic men who tempt as they shout: "Come Down and we will believe." "Come Down from your belief in the Heavenly Father." "Come Down from your belief in Divinity." "Come Down from the cross and we will believe." Jesus could have believers if He would give up the Cross, but without the Cross, Jesus could not be the Saviour.

But as He did not fall down before Satan, neither did He come down from the cross, for perfect love is the choice of Divine Love. He would choose the Father's Will either to this wealth or His bodily comfort. And that is why: "Greater love than this no man hath, that he lay down His life for his friend."

Now His love was not just declared by word, but proven by deed. He could enjoy the fruit of perfect love: "Father, into Thy Hands I commend My Spirit."

For us, there can be but one conclusion: it is not enough to bear a Christian name, we must also merit the name. "Not everyone that saith 'Lord, Lord' shall enter into the Kingdom of heaven." We can prove we love Our Lord only by choosing Him in preference to anything else. The condition of returning to the Father's hands on the last day is the choice of His Cross and all that it implies.

At any moment of our existence, we can test whether we are truly Christian, and that test will be the obedience to His commandments: "He that hath my commandments and keepeth them, he it is that loveth me. And he that loveth me shall be loved of my Father, and I will love him and manifest myself to him. And my Father will love him, and we will come to him and make our abode with him" (John 14: 21-23).

This brings us to the second lesson of Charity. In this Seventh Word, Our Lord did not express Love of the Father in terms of keeping commandments: it was a personal relationship; that of Father and Son. Even in the text: "He that loveth my commandments and keepeth them, he it is that loveth me," the possessive adjective is to be noted. The commandments are not abstract laws separable from His Person; they are one with Him.

"If you love Me keep My commandments." Perfect love is therefore quite distinct from obedience to commandments as laws. Laws are for the imperfect; love is for the perfect. Law is for those who want to know the minimum; love is for those who are interested in the maximum. Laws, therefore, are generally negative: "Thou shalt not . . ."; love is affirmative: "Love the Lord, thy God, with thy whole heart."

Imperfect Christians are concerned only with keeping the laws of the Church; they want to know how far they can go without committing a mortal sin; how near they can get to hell without falling in; how much wrong they can do short of punishment; how they can please God without displeasing themselves.

The perfect Christian is never interested in borders, or the minimum because love is never measured. Mary Magdalene did not count out the drops of the precious ointment as she poured them on the feet of Our Divine Saviour. Judas did; he counted the cost.

But Magdalene, because she loved, broke the vessel and gave everything, for love has no limits. St. Paul, in like manner, could think of no better way of describing the love of Christ for sinners than to say: "He emptied himself."

There is no law that those who love should give gifts to their beloved; there are no laws that mothers should love children. Where there is love, there is no law, because love has no limits.

There was no boundary to the cross; the arms outstretched even into infinity portrayed the universal efficacy of Redemption. There was no counting the cost: "Not my will but Thine be done." He even refused to touch a drink which might have dulled His senses, and thus deprive His will of complete self-devotion for men.

Like Magdalene, He broke the chalice of His Life, and poured out "plentiful Redemption." Such perfect love could be compensated only by a return to perfect love: "Father, into Thy Hands I commend My Spirit."

The essence of Christianity is love, yes! But not love as our world understands it; not loving those who love us, but loving even those who hate us. Love is not in the organism, but in the will; not in affection, but in intention; not in satisfaction, but in preference to the choosing of God above everything.

Every soul then, even those who irritate, annoy and hate us must be looked upon as a potential lover of Christ, and every Christian must be regarded as a kind of consecrated host.

The most degraded man on the face of the earth is precious, and Christ died for Him. That poor soul may have made the wrong choice, but that is not for us to decide. While he has life, he has hope. He might not seem lovable to us, but he is loved by God.

The perfection of all virtue is charity; love of God and love of our neighbor. Whether or not we, like Christ, shall deliver our soul into the Father's hands on the last day, depends entirely upon the use we make of our freedom.

When we abuse it, our conscience tells us that we are our own worst enemy. "Now I know that when I nailed thee to a Cross, it was my own heart I slew." All sin is self-mutilation.

Most of us are kept back from a perfect love of God, "... fearful lest having Him, we should have naught else beside." There is a fear of losing something by obedience to Him; a hesitation of venturing all on God. Could we but see that when we have the sun we need not the candle, then all would be easy.

God grant us the light to see that in loving Him we have everything, and with that light, the grace to die with His words on our lips: "Father, into Thy Hands I commend My Spirit."

ACKNOWLEDGMENTS

To the members of the Archbishop Fulton John Sheen Foundation in Peoria, Illinois. In particular, to the Most Rev. Daniel R. Jenky, C.S.C., Bishop of Peoria, for your leadership and fidelity to the cause of Sheen's canonization and the creation of this book.

www.archbishopsheencause.org

To the staff at Sophia Institute Press for their invaluable assistance in sharing the writings of Archbishop Fulton J. Sheen to a new generation of readers.

www.sophiainstitute.com

To the volunteers at the Archbishop Fulton J. Sheen Mission Society of Canada: your motto "Unless Souls are Saved, Nothing is Saved", speaks to the reality that Jesus Christ came into the world to make salvation available to all souls.

www.archbishopfultonjsheenmissionsocietyofcanada.org

To the good folks at 'Bishop Sheen Today'. We value your guidance, support, and prayers in helping us to share the wisdom of Archbishop Fulton J. Sheen. Your apostolic work of sharing his audio and video presentations along with his many writings to a worldwide audience is very much appreciated.

www.bishopsheentoday.com

And lastly, to Archbishop Fulton J. Sheen, whose teachings on Our Lord's Passion and His Seven Last Words continue to inspire me to love God more and to appreciate the gift of the Church. May we be so blessed as to imitate Archbishop Sheen's love for the saints, the sacraments, the Eucharist, and the Blessed Virgin Mary. May the Good Lord grant him a very high place in heaven!

ABOUTH THE AUTHOR

Fulton J. Sheen
(1895–1979)

ARCHBISHOP SHEEN, best known for his popularly televised and syndicated television program, Life is Worth Living, is held today as one of Catholicism's most widely recognized figures of the twentieth century.

Fulton John Sheen, born May 8, 1895, in El Paso, Illinois was raised and educated in the Roman Catholic faith. Originally named Peter John Sheen, he came to be known as a young boy by his mother's maiden name, Fulton. He was ordained a priest of the Diocese of Peoria at St. Mary's Cathedral in Peoria, IL on September 20, 1919.

Following his ordination, Sheen studied at the Catholic University of Louvain, where he earned a doctorate in philosophy in 1923. That same year, he received the Cardinal Mercier Prize for International Philosophy, becoming the first-ever American to earn this distinction.

Upon returning to America, after varied and extensive work throughout Europe, Sheen continued to preach and teach theology and philosophy from 1927 to 1950, at the Catholic University of America in Washington DC.

Beginning in 1930, Sheen hosted a weekly Sunday night radio broadcast called 'The Catholic Hour'. This broadcast captured many devoted listeners, reportedly drawing an audience of four million people every week for over twenty years.

In 1950, he became the National Director of the Society for the Propagation of the Faith, raising funds to support missionaries. During the sixteen years that he held this position, millions of dollars were raised to support the missionary activity of the Church. These efforts influenced tens of millions of people all over the world, bringing them to know Christ and his Church. In addition, his preaching and personal example brought about many converts to Catholicism.

In 1951, Sheen was appointed Auxiliary Bishop of the Archdiocese of New York. That same year, he began hosting his television program 'Life is Worth Living', which lasted for six years.

In the course of its run, that program competed for airtime with popular television programs hosted by the likes of Frank Sinatra and Milton Berle. Sheen's program held its own, and in 1953, just two years after its debut, he won an Emmy Award for "Most Outstanding Television Personality." Fulton Sheen credited the Gospel writers - Matthew, Mark, Luke, and John - for their valuable contribution to his success. Sheen's television show ran until 1957, boasting as many as thirty million weekly viewers.

In the Fall of 1966, Sheen was appointed Bishop of Rochester, New York. During that time, Bishop Sheen hosted another television series, 'The Fulton Sheen Program' which ran from 1961 to 1968, closely modeling the format of his 'Life is Worth Living' series.

After nearly three years as Bishop of Rochester, Fulton Sheen resigned and was soon appointed by Pope Paul VI as Titular Archbishop of the See of Newport, Wales. This new appointment allowed Sheen the flexibility to continue preaching.

Another claim to fame was Bishop Sheen's annual Good Friday homilies, which he preached for fifty-eight consecutive years at St. Patrick's Cathedral in New York City, and elsewhere. Sheen also led numerous retreats for priests and religious, preaching at conferences all over the world.

When asked by Pope St. Pius XII how many converts he had made, Sheen responded, "Your Holiness, I have never counted them. I am always afraid that if I did count them, I might think I made them, instead of the Lord."

Sheen was known for being approachable and down to earth. He used to say, "If you want people to stay as they are, tell them what they want to hear. If you want to improve them, tell them what they should know." This he did, not only in his preaching but also through his numerous books and articles. His book titled 'Peace of Soul' was sixth on the New York Times best-seller list.

Three of Sheen's great loves were: the missions and the propagation of the faith; the Holy Mother of God and the Eucharist.

He made a daily holy hour of prayer before the Blessed Sacrament. It was from Jesus Himself that he drew strength and inspiration to preach the gospel, and in the Presence of Whom that he prepared his homilies. "I beg [Christ] every day to keep me strong physically and alert mentally, in order to preach His gospel and proclaim His Cross and Resurrection," he said. "I am so happy doing this that I sometimes feel that when I come to the good Lord in Heaven, I will take a few days' rest and then ask Him to allow me to come back again to this earth to do some more work."

His contributions to the Catholic Church are numerous and varied, ranging from educating in classrooms, churches, and homes, to preaching over a nationally-publicized radio show, and two television programs, as well as penning over sixty written works. Archbishop Fulton J. Sheen had a gift for communicating the Word of God in the most pure, simple way. His strong background in philosophy helped him to relate to everyone in a highly personalized manner. His timeless messages continue to have great relevance today. His goal was to inspire everyone to live a God-centered life with the joy and love that God intended.

On October 2, 1979, Archbishop Sheen received his greatest accolade, when Pope St. John Paul II embraced him at St. Patrick's Cathedral in New York City. The Holy Father said to him, "You have written and spoken well of the Lord Jesus. You are a loyal son of the Church."

The good Lord called Fulton Sheen home on December 9, 1979. His television broadcasts now available through various media, and his books, extend his earthly work of winning souls for Christ. Sheen's cause for canonization was opened in 2002. In 2012, Pope Benedict XVI declared him 'Venerable', and in July of 2019, Pope Francis formally approved the miracle necessary for Sheen's beatification and canonization process to move forward. The time and date for the church to declare Archbishop Fulton J. Sheen a saint is in God's hands.

J.M.J.

Books Available Through Bishop Sheen Today Publishing

The Seven Last Words

Calvary and the Mass

The Holy Hour Prayer Book

The Cross and the Beatitudes

The Cross and the Crisis

Missions and the World Crisis

The Seven Last Words of Christ Explained

Father, Forgive Them for They Know Not What They Do.

This Day Thou Shall Be with Me in Paradise

Woman Behold Your Son; Behold Your Mother

My God! My God! Why Hast Thou Forsaken Me?

I Thirst

It is Finished

Father Into Your Hands I Commend My Spirit

Love One Another

The Divine Verdict

God Love You

The Seven Last Words Explained

The Priest Is Not His Own

The Cross and the Crib

Philosophies at War

Seven Words to the Cross

Seven Pillars of Peace

Love One Another

Seven Words of Jesus & Mary

Victory Over Vice

The Seven Virtues

For God and Country

God and War

Liberty, Equality and Fraternity

The Rainbow of Sorrow

www.BISHOPSHEENTODAY.com